Discovering
ENGLISH FURNITURE
1500—1720

John Bly

Line drawings by Robin Ollington

Shire Publications, Tring, Herts.

By the same author

Discovering Hallmarks on English Silver
Discovering English Furniture 1720-1830

CONTENTS

This is the first of three volumes by John Bly describing the development of English furniture. The second title 'Discovering English Furniture 1720-1830' has been published. The third title 'Discovering Victorian and Edwardian Furniture' is in preparation.

INTRODUCTION

The story of old English furniture has in the past been divided into four main periods up to the beginning of the nineteenth century—those of Oak, Walnut, Mahogany and Satinwood. Furniture made between 1800 and 1830 is generally known as Regency, although the political Regency lasted only from 1811 to 1820. The term Regency drifts somewhat obscurely into William IV and Victorian, for it is only during the last fifteen years that any serious study has been made of this interim period, and still more recently of the Victorian itself.

The subject is both simple and complex. Simple because the stages of acquiring a basic knowledge follow a pattern related to the development of the industry itself, and complex because the periods of change or transition are directly linked with the economic, political, international and social development of our history. While it is true that all domestic articles reflect to some degree the disposition of people at any given time, furniture is the one commodity to be found in every household since our earliest civilisations. Therefore a study of English furniture is made much easier if accompanied by an understanding of the life and times of the period in question. The history of English furniture is a development: one method of construction led to another; one design formed the basis for another or created a demand for change. Either the natural invention of the craftsman or influence from abroad and the other factors mentioned above were responsible for these changes.

So it is impossible to understand fully any one period of English furniture without first knowing something of its background. A study of Victorian furniture encompasses Elizabethan, Gothic, Rustic, and New Sheraton designs as well as the French, Italian, and other 'typical' Victorian styles. These cannot truly be recognised unless something is known of the original, which in turn evolved from an earlier style or was caused by a specific reason and made in a way peculiar to that time, taking into consideration the materials available or in vogue and the tools at hand. The basic ground knowledge is simple, the pattern can be learnt. But once over the threshold, complexity begins, and the study of just one designer or maker, of one type of article or of one period can easily become a lifetime's interest. The study of English furniture is always stimulating. It can also be completely absorbing for one reason—no one person has ever, and will ever, know it all.

THE SIXTEENTH CENTURY

Tudor 1500-1558

The population in England in 1500 was just under five million —less than the number of people living in the Greater London area today and approximately one-tenth of our present population. We were over halfway through the reign of Henry VII (1485-1509), the first of the Tudors, and had yet to experience the rule of Henry VIII (1509-1547) and the monumental breakaway from the Church of Rome. The Reformation was a regrettable period when churches throughout the land were desecrated and the fittings, windows, memorials, floors and wall paintings were destroyed. So too were many of the early Nottingham alabaster figures and thousands of ounces of fine silverware. For many centuries we had had an extremely high standard of craftsmanship in building and decorating, but this had for the main part been applied to the Church. Under the feudal system, which existed until the late fifteenth and early sixteenth centuries, personal fortunes were quickly gained and lost. Much depended on physical strength and the ability to rouse some local inhabitants to take up arms against an unfriendly neighbour, and the larger houses were built as strongly fortified as possible.

Therefore, the pre-Elizabethan furniture in this country was sparse and basically utilitarian. The bed, the most important household article at this time, the chest, the table and benches had to be moved sometimes in haste because of an all too frequent house fire or a sudden attack. Wealth was displayed by the fineness of the banners and other wall hangings, the amount of silverware and gold on display, and the quality of the blankets on the bed. All of these could be packed quickly into the chest and carried to safety, the rest of the furniture being made either collapsible and portable, or expendable.

What decoration there was on domestic furniture had for centuries taken its theme from ecclesiastic style and design like the arch shapes of doors and windows. This was done by carving in low relief, Fig. 1, chip carving, or by decorating with bright paint. A fine example of chip carving, i.e. cutting away the surface of the wood in small regular chunks so as to form the pattern, can be seen in Plate 1. The more common use of this type of carving was on the outer edges of the early chests, the main parts being left plain. Examples of this type of chest can still be found today, but fine ones are rare. The paint used on furniture followed the application of a grain filler, see Gesso page 25, and was a kind of tempera.

The Church style decoration continued—certainly in rural

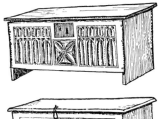

Fig. 1: A five board chest, showing low relief carving in the Gothic style popular until the period of the Reformation, and sometimes used in conjunction with the medallion heads or arcaded fronts of the Renaissance styles thereafter until the latter part of the sixteenth century.

Fig. 2: A five board chest showing the medallion head carved decoration popular during the early Renaissance in England, the first half of the sixteenth century.

England—well into the sixteenth century, and is described as Gothic. By the early sixteenth century, however, another pattern had become popular. This was the carving of chest fronts with medallion heads, Fig. 2.

Religious persecution and general unrest continued under the Council of Regency of the young Edward VI (1547-1553) who was only sixteen when he died, and the short reign of Queen Mary (1553-1558). But by now feudalism was dead and instead of fighting amongst themselves the warring barons joined in the seemingly endless campaigns on the Continent. Here it was found that the French, during their invasions into Italy, had noted that the Italians were reappraising their earlier art forms, and subsequently had introduced to the courts of France a contemporary Italian style. As this was a revival of previous designs, the French called it the Renaissance.

Naturally, new ideas of design filtered back to England, and because ecclesiastical design was at a standstill, our craftsmen turned their skills to domestic work. During the latter part of the sixteenth century they were encouraged by a more peaceful England and a home life more as we know it today. One example of direct Italian Renaissance influence was the shape of the Savonarola folding chair, Fig. 3. The original was designed and made for Girolamo Savonarola, a Dominican friar introduced to Florence by Lorenzo Medici and who, ironically, was to preach strongly against the Medici family and the Renaissance while still under Lorenzo's patronage. English chairs of the sixteenth century in the shape of the savonarola are extremely rare, but the chair was much copied during the latter part of the nineteenth century.

Until the seventeenth century most English furniture was

made of oak, the rest being cottage furniture of the more remote parts of the country where ash, elm, beech or anything else that was readily available might have been used. Unfortunately, being less durable than oak, hardly any early English fruitwood furniture has survived. The oak used was not English oak,

Fig. 3: A 'Savonarola' folding chair. Similar chairs are referred to in English manuscripts of the sixteenth century, following the appearance of the 'Savonarola' in Italy during the time of the Renaissance. Original examples are extremely rare, but the design was much copied during the Victorian period.

Fig. 4: A five board seat typical of the early sixteenth century. Clearly shown are the heads of either wooden pegs or hand-made iron nails securing the joints.

however. This, with its natural stout curving branches and short trunk, was thought suitable only for building ships and houses. Instead we imported oak from Norway and the Baltic countries. Furniture construction was a basic plank or slab method, the five board seat being a typical example, Fig. 4. Two equal pieces of wood formed each end, two more formed the front and back, and a fifth made the seat or top. The two ends were often cut with a large inverted V to make four simple feet and the joints were secured with large hand-made nails or pegs. The dining table was merely two or three long planks joined to form a top, resting on two or three trestles. In winter the fire was built in the centre of the main hall, the smoke drifting up to the large barnlike roof to escape where it could, and the dining table was placed along the side of the hall. The master and lady of the house sat at the centre of the table with their guests and members of the household on their right and left respectively, all facing the fire. With the exception of the hosts, who had simple box-like seats with high backs and solid arms, everyone sat on stools or benches, using the wall for support.

The chest, second to the bed in importance, was used in many ways. It could stand in the dining room for use as an additional seat, and there are records of some with the tops inset with contrasting coloured woods to make chessboards. Invariably there was a chest at the foot of the bed to hold linen or, as one early manuscript suggests, the occasional lover.

The bed itself was the most sophisticated piece of furniture in the house. The four rails which formed the frame were bored with regularly spaced holes. Ropes were then threaded through and stretched across from side to side and from head to foot, thus making a pliant and strong base for the mattress. This was filled with rushes and wool or, in the better houses, feathers and down. Over the mattress went the finest wool sheets and blankets.

During the fifteenth century a method of setting a thin plank of wood within a framework of thicker pieces had been devised. The joints of the frame were made with a tongue on one piece fitting into a precut slot in the other, known as a mortice and tenon joint (mortesse and tennant *sic*). The joints were dry —without glue—and allowed sufficient movement for the wood to expand and contract without cracking, but were tight enough to stop the whole thing falling apart. The next step was to peg these joints. Before final construction one or two holes were bored in the mortice and tenon parts slightly off centre from

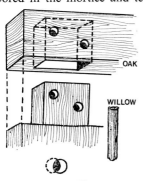

Fig. 5: The construction of a mortice and tenon joint. Originally called a 'mortesse and tennant' the latter part fitted into a precut slot in which one or two holes had been bored. The tenon was marked, removed, and then bored with two holes off centre from those in the mortice. When placed together again split willow pegs were driven in to secure the joint.

each other so that when joined in place an incomplete circle could be seen when looking through the joint, Fig. 5. Into these holes willow pegs were driven, thus drawing the two parts tightly together. Willow was used because it has a long fibrous grain, and when split (not cut) into pegs and driven into position in a pegged joint it is almost impossible to break. The use of panelling and joining in the construction of furniture continued well into the seventeenth century, and the man responsible for the frame making was known as a 'joyner'. Hence our early 'joyned' or joint stools, Fig. 6. A guide, but not a rule, to the authenticity of an early piece of furniture made in this way is the fact that the ends of the pegs which were driven in from the outside, were rarely cut off inside, and protrude anything up to half an inch inside the frame. This applies to the underside of seat rails and other places where, with normal use, they would not be seen or cause an obstruction.

Fig. 6: A 'joyned' or joint stool of the type dating from the early 1600s. The pegged joints are clearly visible, as are the ends of the pegs on the top. All external peg ends may protrude fractionally, see 'Wood Behaviour' page 55. Joint stools were most popular during the seventeenth century.

Elizabethan, 1558-1603

With the accession of Queen Elizabeth I (1558-1603), England faced a period of internal peace and progress. General prosperity spread through the country, and a new middle class of tradesmen and businessmen emerged. Large family houses were no longer peculiar to the titled and landed gentry. Houses were built for stable and secure family life, and the pattern of class distinction as it was known until the early twentieth century was set. Servants and other members of the household no longer took food, wine, and enjoyed entertainment with the master and his family. They had their own quarters, which in time became very important to the furniture industry in this country. And so with different patterns of life developed different patterns of furniture.

The dining hall became much more as we would recognise it today. The fire was built into the wall and the dining table placed in the middle of the room. Although still the same long rectangular shape, the supports were now four or six bulbous, turned legs, Fig. 7, built into a frame with horizontal members, called

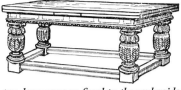

Fig. 7: An Elizabethan extending dining table on 'double cup' or 'cup and cover' turned and carved supports. This shape is repeated on contemporary bed posts and on the front supports on buffets and court cupboards. The two ends of the lower top each have two long runners fixed to the underside; when pulled out the weight of the full length top rests on these runners and supports the two leaves. This type of dining table was popular throughout the seventeenth century, the turned legs becoming progressively more slender.

stretchers, six to eight inches from the floor and the same at the top forming a frieze rail or apron. On finer furniture the rails were often decorated with carving or simple types of inlay. The stools and benches were often made and decorated to match the table and were placed all round it. To compensate for the lack of a wall to lean against a back was built on to each stool and thus the dining chair became established as an article of domestic furniture.

As furniture became more ornate and diverse in use, more skill was needed in its manufacture. Considering the tools available, joiners were capable of high degrees of accuracy in

Fig. 8: A country turner's pole lathe. A young springy tree was either used where it grew or was cut and set at an angle to be worked through a hole in the roof of the turner's shed. Turning by this method continued in some rural areas throughout the nineteenth century.

joining, pegging, carving and turning. This applied more to the country craftsmen, for in London and other major cities joining, turning and carving were mostly separate occupations. In rural areas turning was done with a pole lathe, Fig. 8. A young springy tree was cut and set at an angle with a rope attached to its tip. The end of the rope was joined to a thinner cord. The piece of timber to be turned was mounted in a simple lathe, the cord wound around it and the end attached to a treadle on the floor. The spring in the tree pulled the rope up, and pressure on the treadle pulled it down, causing the piece of wood to spin first one way and then the other. Turning by this method continued in some parts of England until well into the nineteenth century, and the majority of pre-1800 fruitwood, yew and beech turned parts, such as legs, stretchers, spindles for chair backs and cupboard door panels, Fig. 9, were made in this way.

Fig. 9: A food cupboard with panels of turned spindles forming grill doors. Dating from the late sixteenth/early seventeenth centuries, this type of cupboard was made, certainly in rural areas, for the next two hundred years with slight modifications according to contemporary decoration.

By the end of the sixteenth century our houses were becoming quite full of hitherto little known articles of furniture. Food cupboards with doors that swung open on two iron pin pivots became popular, many with panels of turned spindles forming a grill, Fig. 9. These were usually at eye level and supported on another cupboard base or on four turned legs with a drawer in the frieze. There were endless variations on this idea of a cupboard on a stand, the two most popular being the buffet or court cupboard and the hall cupboard, Fig. 10. A feature common to nearly all this type of cupboard furniture is that the top part was set back a little to form a narrow shelf, while the top rail protrudes in line with the base to form a canopy. In early pieces this was supported by a bulbous turned column at each front corner, probably matching the turned legs of the dining table, stools and chairs. During the seventeenth century these columns tended to be cut off, leaving a canopy with a large turned pendant drop at each front corner. The earlier design was often made to match the bed posts. Elizabethan beds were highly decorated with carving, having two turned posts at the foot supporting a canopy extending from the high, panelled head board. This was hung with fine cloth drapes and tapestry curtains, Fig. 11. So by the turn of the sixteenth century we had reached the age of the well appointed household and were about to embark on one of the most important and exciting periods in the history of furniture.

Fig. 10: An oak hall cupboard showing the turned pendants below the canopy. The more usual form on seventeenth century examples is the use of full turned columns in this position. Their function can be attributed to the earlier court and hall cupboards wherein the two end panels of the top half receded at an angle from the front centre section thus forming a splay front effect; the columns thus supporting the canopy as well as being decorative. The shaped panels of the lower half of this cupboard are peculiar to the middle and late eighteenth century as are the 'swan-neck' handles. Most oak cupboard furniture made during the seventeenth and eighteenth centuries can be dated in this way.

Fig. 11: An Elizabethan bed showing the bulbous turned front supports similar to those on tables and cupboards of the period. It continued with these proportions from 1600 until the early eighteenth century.

Jacobean, 1603-1625

The accession of James I of England, James VI of Scotland, began what we know as the Jacobean period. James I was the first king of a legally united kingdom but, unlike many of his successors, he had little personal effect on the styles of furniture and design generally. He was overfond of hunting and drinking, preoccupied with religious discontent and not concerned with tastes and fashions. He therefore contributed little to the development of furniture. It was mainly influence from the Continent, coupled with the inventiveness of our own craftsmen that supplied new and more advanced methods of meeting the needs of society. Furniture became more ornate, with frequent use of deeper carving. One significant change in a particular motif was the gradual elongation of the bulbous 'double cup' or 'cup and cover', turning it into a more vase-like shape, see Fig. 12, C and D. Concurrent with this change was another new and popular motif known today as 'bobbin turning', see Fig. 12, A and B. This gives the appearance of a number of balls joined together in a straight line, sometimes interspersed with rings. It demanded a careful choice of timber, for although first used for legs and rails only, complete chairs were soon made with every member turned in this pattern and long grained wood was needed for strength. It was found also that pieces of bobbin-turned wood could be cut in half and then applied to the carcase —the basic framework of chest furniture—as well as to drawer fronts and cupboard doors.

From the simple drawer sliding in and out on the carcase frame and the drawer bottom, were developed the highly efficient side 'runners'. During the early seventeenth century the utility value of a piece of furniture with several sliding drawers became apparent, but when the drawers were full their weight caused them to rub on the supporting rail in the carcase. So the drawer bottom was made to extend beyond the width of the drawer, the resultant two 'lips' running in slots cut into the carcase. To hide the slots when the drawer was in place the drawer front was made larger than the opening in the carcase. Soon, however, two proper drawer runners were added. Each of these was a strip of hard wood, approximately $\frac{3}{8}$in. x $\frac{1}{2}$in., placed in the carcase midway between the top and bottom of the drawer opening at each side and running from front to back. A groove, called a rabbet, was then worked into the sides of the drawer to accommodate the runner and the problem was solved, see Plate 2. Previously seldom used in anything other than the base

A   B   C   D   E

Fig. 12: Five types of turned and carved supports used on chairs, stools and tables during the seventeenth century. The following approximate dates are when these designs were most popular. (a) Knob or bobbin turning, 1630-1675. (b) Ball and ring or bobbin turning, 1640-1675. (c) Double cup or cup and cover, often carved with fluting, 1580-1690. (d) Fluted baluster, 1600-1700. (e) Pillar, 1605-1675.

parts of buffets, a single long drawer, or two short drawers side by side were now being built into the bases of chest furniture.

The development of putting first one drawer and then another above, thus providing more drawer space and less chest, was the beginning of the chest of drawers, popular from the early eighteenth century to the present day.

The use of sliding parts in furniture also gave us the extending or draw leaf dining table. First introduced during the late sixteenth century, this type of table became popular in the Jacobean period. Variations of the draw leaf construction were produced throughout the ensuing periods to the present day, and many of our modern extending tables work on the same basic principle as the Elizabethan version, see Fig. 7. When closed the table looks like a refectory or long dining table with a double top on a rectangular frame supported by four turned legs. The top lifts up and from each end a leaf of timber the same width and almost half the length of the top is pulled out. Each of these leaves has attached to the underside two 'lopers' or extended runners the same length as the table. When both leaves are pulled out the centre part drops down level with the two leaves and its weight pressing on the four lopers supports the two ends.

By the beginning of the Jacobean period a crude form of inlay,

15

of which there are some records during the late sixteenth century, had gained recognition. The piece of wood to be decorated had drawn on to it a pattern, usually of stylised flowers, vines, tendrils and leaves, which was then cut out of the wood to a depth of up to a quarter of an inch. The same shapes were then formed with other materials such as ivory, mother of pearl, woods of holly, box and ebony, and the pieces let in to the first piece of wood. The use of this type of inlay developed from small panels to general decoration for rails, friezes, frames, etc., with either the scrolled vine motif or with small symmetrical pieces of wood in alternating colours applied in bands called chequer inlay.

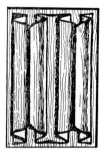 

Fig. 13: Two panels of carved 'linen fold'. Introduced to England during the second quarter of the sixteenth century and of Flemish origin, it was popular during the remainder of the century; extant contemporary English examples are fairly plain. It was much used for decoration during the Victorian age.

Inlay decoration was used in conjunction with carving, turning and, by the 1620s, the 'moulded front' on drawer, door and chest panels. As we have seen, the practice of carving the panels on the front and sides of furniture was by this time well established, and one consistently fashionable design during the sixteenth and early seventeenth centuries was the 'linen fold', see Fig. 13. The panel is carved in low relief to give the appearance of a carefully folded piece of cloth solidified and applied to the panel, the effect of this being to raise or bring out the centre of the panel while the four sides recede into the framework. Continuing and elaborating on this raised effect was the moulded front, Plate 3. The drawer was set back in the carcase frame, say, three-quarters of an inch. Four strips of wood were then applied round the edge forming a frame. The strips were of triangular section, and the longest side was moulded or grooved. Another piece of wood of the same proportions as the drawer front, but smaller, was then applied to the centre. This piece might be up to one and a half inches thick and was framed with more moulding; in the centre of this went the metal handle. The more elaborate chests of the 1620-1640 period had many complex variations on this symmetrical moulded theme. A typical example is the chest with one long deep drawer moulded to simulate two short drawers above two cupboard doors similarly decorated and enclosing three plain fronted drawers, Plate 4. The two doors were secured by an iron lock and swung open on iron hinges. A substantial piece of moulding was then added immediately below the drawer or door opening at the base of the carcase to balance the overhanging top and the whole article was raised from the floor by the elongated upright members of the carcase.

By the early 1620s an improved method of joining the front panel to the sides of drawers had been devised, the back joints being secured with iron nails in the established manner. This method was known as 'dove-tailing' from the shape of the parts and counterparts to be joined, Plate 2, and on the earliest or provincial examples of dovetailing the joints were strengthened with iron pins driven through the ends, also Plate 2. However, the rapid advance of joiners' skill and the introduction of new materials during the following twenty years dispensed with the need for this nailing on the finest furniture, but it can sometimes be found on country-made pieces as late as the beginning of the eighteenth century.

Charles I, 1625-1649

Charles I, unlike James I, had immense personal influence on style and fashion, and was responsible for many of the revolutionary changes in our pattern of living. His marriage to Henrietta, daughter of Henry IV of France, increased continental influence on design, fashion and etiquette. Charles I was not only a connoisseur and a patron of art, he was the first recognised collector of works of art from other countries as well as England. He was fond of and advocated reading, hitherto confined to lay scholars and the clergy, and he encouraged the development of trade with Europe and the Middle and Far East through our own East India Company. This company had been incorporated by Royal Charter in 1600 to compete with the Dutch merchants for trade in lands beyond the Cape of Good Hope or the Straits of Magellan. Thus began an age of great commercial expansion.

We were importing fine porcelain from China, glass from Venice, pottery from Delft in Holland, spices and peppers from the East Indies, fine cloth from Damascus and Italy, chests or trunks from Japan decorated with the gum of the lac tree and known as Japanned work or lacquer, all of which were to have important influence on the development of English furniture. As the requirements of household furniture became rapidly more diverse, more accuracy was necessary in its manufacture, and coinciding with this was the more general use of walnut, much of which was imported from Spain and the south of France. Walnut, which until the latter part of the seventeenth century was used in the solid, had a much closer grain than oak, and could therefore be cut more exactly. When rubbed well down by hand polishing it showed great depth of colour and extremely attractive markings. By this time we were beginning to use imported fabric and fine leather to cover the seats and backs of chairs. Apart from the Court and wealthier households, covered chairs were generally regarded as bedroom articles, being too costly for the rigours of everyday use. The examples of covered chairs of the Charles I period that can be said to have been designed for use outside the bedroom are those of square and solid shape, and with a low back. This was to accommodate the arm of the gentleman as he sat sideways, encumbered by his sword. The practice of leaving personal armament in the ante-room did not start until the early eighteenth century. Also the back legs of chairs had, during this period, become permanently splayed out to counteract the inborn habit of all generations to tip back.

Although we were covering chairs with various fabrics, upholstery, i.e. padding and stuffing before covering, was rare before 1645 and it was to become even more rare in the immediate future. We had begun to experiment and expand in many fields—trade, commerce, sacred and secular architectural design, exploration—when the country was divided by the Civil War. This outwardly ended with the execution of Charles I and the exile to France of his two sons, Charles and James. The eleven year Commonwealth which followed, under the rule of Oliver Cromwell, 1649-1660, was a period of overriding religious zeal, and the development and advancement of design was curbed.

Commonwealth, 1649-1660

Puritan beliefs of this period decreed righteousness in self-denial, and furniture made in the Midlands and south of England during the Commonwealth reflects this feeling. The 1650s were notoriously dull years as far as furniture is concerned, and everything that could be associated with gracious living was discouraged. All goods and chattels were made to be strictly functional, without unnecessary adornment, with precious little comfort, and lacking in artistic sensibility.

But at least two men during this period were working on experiments that were to create new exercises for the skills of our craftsmen in the near future. As early as 1643 Evangelista Torricelli, while working on a theory by Galileo, had discovered that the external atmosphere controls the power of a vacuum inside a sealed tube. If a glass tube has a measured amount of mercury—a non-evaporative liquid—poured into it and is then sealed, the rise and fall of the mercury will indicate the external atmosphere or barometric pressure. Torricelli was unfortunately hampered by the lack of sufficiently advanced materials, the most important being suitable glass tubing, but we were well on the way to the first domestic barometer. The other man was Christian Huygens, a Dutchman, who in 1657 discovered the importance of the applied pendulum. This was originally yet another of Galileo's theories, but he had used it only in the research of oscillations. By giving a pendulum momentum by means of power from a weight on a chain or specially woven rope over a toothed wheel and correcting the length of the arc of its swing by means of a mechanical escapement, it was possible to achieve accuracy with a timepiece movement. Thus began the development of the clock, which soon became popular in the finer houses all over England, see Fig. 14.

Restoration and Carolean, 1660-1685

Charles II landed at Dover in May, 1660, and was crowned at Westminster in April, 1661. In 1662 he married Catherine of Braganza. He was quick witted, a man of great and varied knowledge, and a shrewd judge of men. From Holland he

Fig. 14: A walnut veneered long case clock, c. 1700. This artist's impression is intended to show the elaborate extremes achieved by cabinet makers for this relatively new household article by 1700. By this time cases of the same outline but with less ornate decoration were being made in various parts of Britain. From 1695 to 1720 marquetry, and from 1700 to 1725 lacquer work, were popular types of decoration for clock cases.

brought a mistress—Louise de Kerouaille—who later became the Duchess of Portsmouth, and in England he found Nell Gwynn. He loved his children, his dogs, his ducks and his Navy. He enjoyed theatre-going, horse racing and gambling, while at the same time patronising the arts and encouraging further trade with Europe and the East. The best social and court biographies of this period are the diaries of Samuel Pepys, but the inclusion

19

here of a brief mention of some of Charles II's interests illustrates one reason why so many innovations in the design and uses of furniture came to be crammed together in such a short period. What Charles patronised in social life, his courtiers, the noblemen, landed gentry and so on down the social scale followed as far as their means would allow. A general interest in the arts developed. People started collecting china, pottery and glass. As these collections grew, and clocks and barometers became more fashionable, a new type of furniture was needed to house them—case and cabinet furniture. With the import of

Fig. 15: *A walnut framed cane panel chair typical of the James II period. The tall narrow back with the cane panel between turned supports was popular after 1685 until the end of the century. The variety of foreign designs appearing in England at this time was incorporated in crestings, stretchers, rails, legs and back supports, making this type of chair particularly interesting and possible to date with accuracy.*

Fig. 16: *A chair rail of bow form of the 1680s, shown here with the scroll or Braganza foot. During this period, the H stretcher on this type of frame chair was sometimes replaced by an elaborate curving X.*

glass from Venice (and one or two highly prized secrets concerning its manufacture) it became obvious that the panels in the doors of cupboards should be of glass instead of wood, thus displaying the prized collections at the same time as protecting them from dust and breakage. The old method of joining and allowing room for the wood to 'move' proved inadequate for glass panels, which did not need to expand and contract, and therefore frames had to be constructed with joints cut to a higher degree of accuracy. The demand for case furniture became so great that a new craftsman emerged, a man specialising in the manufacture of case and cabinet furniture—the cabinet maker.

In 1663, George Villiers, second Duke of Buckingham, secured the sole right to manufacture mirror plates of silvered glass which he unjustly claimed was a process hitherto unknown in England. He started a factory at Vauxhall, and brought over glassmakers from Italy, then the centre of the glass industry, but his discovery was soon to affect the craftsmen of England. Several other patents and monopolies appear to have been granted at the same time, and as the output of mirror glasses grew so did the need for decorative frames to surround them. Many materials were used, such as metal, ivory, tortoiseshell and even needlework over a wood base, but the most popular to emerge was the wood frame intricately pierced and cut by the carver and later decorated by the gilder, see page 25 and Plate 5.

During the 1660s we began importing large quantities of cane from the East, which when woven and strung across the open

Fig. 17: An oak settle of plain panelled construction. These were made in the provinces in this form from the second quarter of the seventeenth century throughout the eighteenth century. Without much decoration, accurate dating of this type of article can be difficult.

seats and backs of chairs provided a greater degree of comfort. Fine examples of cane panel seat furniture made during the last quarter of the seventeenth century can still be found today, see Plate 6. Perhaps the most common is the high back walnut chair which can be used as either a dining or hall chair, see Fig. 15, and which underwent such severe changes in shape as to make it possible to date accurately during the ensuing twenty-five years. The 'H' stretcher frame for chairs became really popular during the early Restoration period, the cross member being slightly more to the front on later examples. Pierced carving on the back top and side rails also became popular, and was adopted for the decoration of the Dutch bow front rail during the 1680s, see Fig. 16. A direct influence from Holland where Charles had spent much of his exile was the Flemish curve which started to appear on the front legs of furniture, especially chairs. This was often combined with the scroll foot, see Fig. 16, known as the 'Braganza Foot', a Spanish influence honouring the Queen.

There were many influences on English design during the Charles II period, with Dutch, Spanish and French appearing from the Continent and, following the great popularity of the merchandise brought over by the East India Company, our first period of 'Chinoiserie'. One reason for the tremendous output of fashionable furniture at this time was the devastating Great Fire of London in September 1665, when 13,200 houses were burnt to the ground. As these were gradually rebuilt, so they were refurnished in the fashionable styles of the day. By the 1670s walnut was considered the standard material for all the finest quality furniture, and our cabinet makers were called upon to manufacture glazed door cabinets, blind (solid wood or mirror plate) door cabinets, cases for clocks and barometers and escritoires; the joiners were producing a new and large variety of tables each for a specific use; and the chair makers and turners were making chairs, day-beds and settles, see Fig. 17. The day-bed, derived from the French chaise-longue, first appeared in England during the early Restoration period. It was made in the same manner as the contemporary chairs, but with a seat that extended forward some five feet, see Fig. 18.

Fig. 18: An early Restoration period day bed, c. 1660. Day beds were introduced in England during the first half of the sixteenth century and had become popular by the early 1600s. After the Restoration, their design closely followed that of the chair, and changes in shapes of chairs can safely be said to apply to day beds of the same period.

Fig. 19: A writing desk or escritoire c. 1695. The two inside front legs swing out and support the sloping 'fall' which is hinged at the bottom front edge. During the early eighteenth century, the box part was placed on a chest of drawers base to make what is now known as a bureau.

22

Fig. 20: A Charles II type of cabinet on stand, c. 1675. Panels of marquetry decorate the door and drawer fronts. Similar decoration was often used on the escritoire cabinet of the period where the two doors are replaced by one large one hinged at the bottom and which opens down to form a writing surface. The semi-circular or oval moulding below the top conceals one long 'secret' drawer.

Through its construction, however, it was not very practicable or long-lasting, and those examples that remain today are not really strong enough for daily use.

During the reign of Charles II the demand grew for smaller articles of furniture made for a specific purpose. One example is the escritoire. A development of the early desk with a sloping top and a forerunner of the bureau, the escritoire was rare in England before the middle of the seventeenth century, but its considerable use is recorded after the Restoration. Basically formed as a desk with a space to accommodate the knees of the writer, and in some instances with a flap that folded in half to form a larger surface, a small drawer was often incorporated in the frieze of the stand, see Fig. 19. The design of the stand inevitably followed the latest developments in the art of the turner. One such development during the Charles II period was the 'barley sugar twist' turning. This design, which is self-descriptive, remained popular in the provinces until well into the eighteenth century, but it had disappeared from the manufacture of fashionable furniture by the early 1700s, see Plate 6. Early barley sugar twist turning was a difficult operation for seventeenth century turners. Largely responsible for much refinement in this craft was the development of the sliding rest. This was a device which enabled the turner to rest his hand and turning chisel on a bracket which slid along parallel with the piece of wood to be turned. Imagine a circular piece of wood mounted in a lathe, and a line gouged along its length from left to right. If the wood had been rotated while the line was being gouged, the result would be a line encircling the wood from end to end. The speed the gouge is drawn from one end to the other together with the speed of the lathe determines the length of the spiral, and either heavy or fine barley sugar turning is produced. This type of turning formed the legs and stretchers

23

of many of the gate leg tables and chairs of the 1660-1685 period, as well as the supports for the chests and cabinets-on-stands which were becoming so popular during this time. A chest containing perhaps a dozen small deep drawers enclosed by two large doors was placed on an open framed stand which might have had a drawer in the frieze, see Fig. 20. Alternatively, the two doors were replaced by one large one that was hinged at the bottom instead of the sides, and so fell down and out, making a writing surface supported by chains or steel arms.

During the early years of the Restoration period oval, round, rectangular and square tables with tops made in three parts became popular. These were a development from the single flap tables of about 1620. The two outside pieces or 'leaves' were attached to the centre with simple iron hinges, folding down when not in use, see Plate 7. The centre part was on a rectangular frame with a leg at each corner and a square frame set in each long side. This swung out on a pivot joint from the main rectangle and, having its then outside upright member the same length as the four main legs, served to support the drop leaf. The name gate-leg has been used to describe this type of table for many years because of its construction, but not all tables of this period had a complete framed 'gate'.

Having dealt briefly with the continental effects on our furniture history, it is advisable to consider the work of the carver and gilder and also the Chinoiserie style in some detail, as all three recur and will be referred to again during the eighteenth and nineteenth centuries. See charts on pages 60 and 61.

The potential skills of the carver developed with the continuance of the use of walnut as seen in the fret or through cutting and shaping on the chairs of the period. But his work

Fig. 21: An agate polisher. This highly polished semi-precious stone replaced for the most part the original dog's tooth used by gilders in England once the decoration of furniture with metal leaf became popular during the latter part of the seventeenth century. It was used to burnish and produce highlights after the gold or silver leaf had been applied.

was even more in demand with the fashion for gilding the surface of carved furniture. As the carved wood was to be covered there was no need to use walnut, and cheaper and softer woods could be used. Pine and lime were found to be excellent for the carvers' work and also for the application of a formula known as gesso prior to the application of the gold or silver leaf itself.

Gesso, which is a combination of pure fine chalk and size made from scrapings of parchment mixed together to make a paste, had been applied to the surface of furniture as a 'grain-filler' prior to decoration since the Middle Ages, but during the seventeenth century its full potential in the hands of a skilled carver became appreciated. The deep open carving was coated with several layers of gesso, each being allowed to dry before the application of the next. This then formed a surface as hard and, when well rubbed down, as smooth as ivory. The carver could then accentuate his work by carving further fine detail into the gesso itself before the article was sent to the gilder. Several coats of burnish size were applied and allowed to harden before the gilder wet the surface with water and then applied the pure gold leaf. As the burnish size quickly absorbed the moisture only small areas could be gilded at one time, thus making the achievement of a consistent colour and surface on large pieces a highly skilled and lengthy process. When the whole had been covered with gold it was rubbed well with a pad, making the surface dull or 'matt'. It was then ready for the finishing stage. Important and often protruding parts of the carving were burnished to a mirror-like surface, thus gaining the 'highlights'. This was done with a dog's tooth or later a polished agate stone correctly shaped and set into a convenient handle, see Fig. 21. The two main methods of gilding furniture are water gilding, described above, and oil gilding. The latter is used more architecturally and on internal and external iron-work and cannot be burnished. It is cheaper, requires less painstaking surface preparation and is generally considered inferior for fine furniture decoration. Fire or mercurial gilding had been used to decorate metals since the Middle Ages. Fine silverware and, during the seventeenth, eighteenth and early nineteenth centuries, metal mounts for furniture were gilded in this way. Mercury and gold will mix and form an amalgam; this is applied to the surface of the metal and the article is then heated. The mercury evaporates and leaves a gold coating. This method is no longer used in England, for the fumes from evaporating mercury are extremely dangerous.

The Chinoiserie taste of the Carolean period made itself apparent in furniture with the considerable use of Japanned or lacquered decoration. Originating in the East, both panels and complete articles of lacquered furniture were imported to this country in vast quantities. To combat this it became expedient that a similar form of decoration should be produced over here. But while we could import as much lacquer work as we wanted, we could not obtain the essential ingredients to make the lacquer, nor had we the right climate or temperament for its application, so the English craftsmen started to copy it as best they could. In 1688, John Stalker and George Parker produced a *Treatise of Japanning and Varnishing*, an important and comprehensive work giving full directions and details concerning surface decoration of furniture. Instead of gum from the lac tree, we used a variety of varnishes and other materials which, it was found, could be turned to considerable advantage. Whereas the background of seventeenth century Oriental lacquer was invariably black, English lacquer of the same period was produced with red, yellow, green and blue backgrounds. The appearance of Japanned work is of scenes wherein the figures, birds, flowers and other main characters are slightly raised from the background surface and then decorated with colour and/or gold leaf.

The methods of making and applying both English and Oriental lacquer are highly technical and space does not allow a comprehensive account in this text, but the fact that the two methods were different has, over the years, presented us with a guide to distinguishing one from the other. During a life span of two hundred and fifty years it is inevitable that the outer surfaces of lacquer furniture has suffered some damage. Where

Fig. 22: An example of a lacquer cabinet on stand of the first Chinoiserie period, c. 1685. Cabinets of this period were either of Oriental origin and purchased through the East India Company at sales held on the docksides of London, or made in England and decorated in imitation by craftsmen and amateurs. The stands were made in England of carved pine, treated with gesso and then applied with metal leaf. See Gesso and Lacquer.

26

seventeenth century English lacquer has chipped and come away from the surface, it has done so in the outline of the raised parts, making obvious the shape and size of the character now missing. Oriental lacquer of the same period tends to come away in irregular sized pieces.

Both English and Oriental lacquer cabinets, enclosed chests and trunks were popular in England until the early 1700s, and the later ones were often placed on specially made carved and gilt wood stands. See Fig. 22.

At the Court of Charles II, gambling had become a fashionable pastime, so the gaming table became one of the new types of furniture required of the joiner. During the last quarter of the seventeenth century card games of loo, basset, ombre and quadrille (ombre for four) were played for high stakes, as well as chess, backgammon and dicing. Card games were played best on tables covered with green cloth or fine needlework. Partly to protect this the tables were made to fold over in half, one or two legs being made to swing out from the frame in the manner of the earlier gate to support the top when open. Also, when closed the table showed a solid wood surface and could stand against the wall to be used as an additional side table. During this period, the East India Company began importing large quantities of chaw, or tea as it is now called, from China. In 1679 the Duchess of Lauderdale is recorded as having a gathering of ladies to sample her chaw in the withdrawing room at Ham House, being probably the first 'tea party', and naturally a table was specially made on which to present the tea. Inevitably the high price of tea at this time kept it within the reach only of the wealthy, and so tea drinking did not seriously affect the designs of furniture until the end of the seventeenth and early part of the eighteenth centuries.

In 1674 George Ravenscroft patented a tough clear glass which essentially founded the domestic glass industry in this country and was to affect furniture in many ways, particularly in the production of barometers and their cases, for it was found that the glass could be drawn into a hollow tube with a one-tenth inch bore. Following the work of Torricelli, Sir Samuel Morland produced in 1670 a signpost barometer, see Fig. 23. The bend in the tube extends about twelve inches and rises off the horizontal about three inches, thereby showing with greater accuracy any atmospheric change along rather than up and down the tube. This type did not gain the popularity expected and the stick or pillar type of case continued to be made with its decoration following the styles of the different periods for the next two hundred years, see Fig. 24. It was superseded in general popularity toward the end of the eighteenth century by the banjo

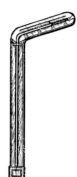

Fig. 23: A signpost barometer. First used in England by Sir Samuel Morland about 1670, the signpost barometer gave greater accuracy of reading 'along' the tube rather than up and down as on the vertical type. However, it never gained the popularity of the vertical or stick barometer though it continued to be made throughout the eighteenth century, its case following to some degree the current designs.

Fig. 24: An example of a Torricellian or cistern barometer. This type, better known today as a stick barometer, works on Torricelli's principle of the mercury resting in a reservoir or cistern at the base of the tube. Stick barometers were popular in the context of furniture design until the second quarter of the eighteenth century, their cases following closely the designs of contemporary clock cases. During the 1770s the siphon or wheel barometer became more fashionable and remained so until well into the nineteenth century. The principle of the wheel barometer, generally known today as a banjo barometer, was first published in 1665 by Dr. Robert Hooke.

or wheel barometer, but returned to favour during the latter part of the nineteenth century.

During the reign of Charles II domestic architecture became a distinct profession; one which had been started in the classical traditions by Inigo Jones (1573-1652) during the first half of the seventeenth century, and which was to affect our furniture design through the work of Daniel Marot during the late seventeenth century and William Kent in the first part of the eighteenth century. Just as real development in all branches of the constructive arts and skills was taking place throughout the country we entered a short period of political unrest and turmoil.

James II, 1685-1689

James II, the second son of Charles I, and his Court had no direct influence on the designs of furniture. Politically he undid much of the good that Charles II had achieved and seemed to have learnt little from the fate of his father. Without direct influence the development of design was for a short time left to the craftsmen. Chair backs were made higher and tended to show a preference for baluster and vase turning, especially on the outside upright members. The seats became narrower, the spaces between the caning became smaller and the work much finer. Otherwise the basic shapes of furniture remained without any significant change and the industry might well have stagnated had we not had an injection of impetus with craftsmen from the Continent. The Revocation of the Edict of Nantes in 1685 deprived the Huguenots (French Protestants) of all civil and religious rights and liberty, and they were forced to flee the country and find sanctuary in Holland and the British Isles. The Huguenots were industrious and highly skilled. They brought to this country new standards of manufacture in woodwork and metalwork (see *Discovering Hall Marks on English Silver*) and new techniques in the weaving of cloth suitable for upholstery. Previously only fine brocades and velvets from Italy and, during the Commonwealth, leather had been used to cover the seats and backs of chairs, but because of their formidable cost and in the case of leather comparative lack of comfort, only on a very small scale. The Government encouraged the weaving of fabric in this country and although the Upholders (later Upholsterers) Guild had been formed prior to 1460, it was not until the end of the seventeenth century that the use of fabric for decoration and comfort and the upholsterer became integral parts of our furniture history.

William and Mary, 1689-1702

The next important development in furniture decoration came with the accession to the throne of England of William III and his wife, Mary II, daughter of James II. William was the son of William, Prince of Orange, who had married Mary, daughter of Charles I. After considerable discontent throughout England with the reign of James II, and following a brief interregnum from 11th December, 1688, to 13th February, 1689, William and Mary were invited to come over from Holland and rule England jointly, the affairs of state being left to William alone. With a Dutch king we naturally had still more influence in our design from the Continent, and with a reigning queen, court and social behaviour again affected the manners and habits of the people. William III brought with him craftsmen skilled in the art of furniture manufacture and we can see evidence of this Dutch influence in both the shape and decoration of much of the better quality household furniture of this post Restoration period. The method of enhancing furniture with thin slices of wood fixed to the surface of the carcase or main body of an article was known as early as the second quarter of the seventeenth century, but it really became popular in England during the 1690s. Now known as veneer it was originally called 'faneer'

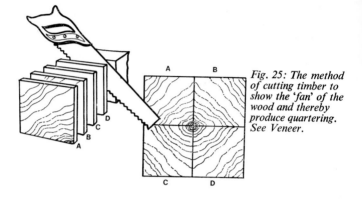

Fig. 25: *The method of cutting timber to show the 'fan' of the wood and thereby produce quartering. See Veneer.*

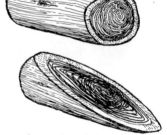

Fig. 26: *The two ways of cutting laburnum to produce (a) rounds and (b) ovals for oyster veneer. See page 30.*

because the slices were cut across the grain of the wood thus showing the 'fan' of the timber, Fig. 25, rather than with the grain, a practice which became popular during the eighteenth century. The term veneer today encompasses the many variations on a theme which quickly developed. Some types were extremely popular for a limited period to be revived at a later date while others continued throughout the eighteenth and nineteenth centuries to the present day. Of the former oyster-shell parquetry and marquetry are the two most important examples. It was found that not only walnut, which was now being imported from France as well as Spain, but also laburnum wood was ideal for veneer. The branches of laburnum were cut at an angle to give oval shapes (oysters) and straight across to give round ones, see Fig. 26. Sometimes the outer ring of sapwood was retained to enhance the oysters of rounds which were then arranged so as to form regular patterns on the surface of the article to be decorated. Interspersing these patterns were lines of box wood, about one-eighth of an inch square in section, known as stringing. Parquetry also applies to any veneering where pieces of wood of contrasting colours are cut and laid so as to form a geometric or symmetric pattern.

The use of marquetry in the form it took during the late seventeenth century was the direct result of the influence of the skills of the Dutch craftsmen. Although a progression from the early type of crude inlay on the carcase to the achievement of this effect with veneers would no doubt have occurred in England anyway, it is accepted that during the reign of William and Mary the latter reached supreme heights of perfection, and the process of decoration known as marquetry became extremely popular.

The basic method of marquetry production is that a number of pieces of veneer cut wood of contrasting colours were glued together one on top of the other with a piece of paper in between each. A piece of rough wood was then placed on the two outer surfaces of the resultant 'sandwich' and on to one of these was pasted a sheet of paper bearing the design of the panel required. The pattern was then cut through with a fine saw blade set at exact right angles to the timbers, the two pieces of rough wood receiving the fraying action of the saw. When the design had been fully cut the woods were separated, using water and a thin bladed knife to work away the paper between each slice. Say four woods were used, there were now four panels, each with a design which could be replaced by three other colours. As walnut was the most popular background, not all the panels were utilised but were kept to be used in the event of breakages in subsequent repeats of the same design. There are two main types of marquetry, being classified as floral and arabesque or seaweed. The first, which is the earlier of the two, incorporated the use of acanthus leaf scrolls, vines, flowers and occasionally birds—parrots or eagles—set in panels surrounded by borders of stringing and crossbanding of walnut or kingwood. For this type a great variety of woods was used. Some were dyed to give additional colours, others were used in their natural state, sometimes being scorched by dipping in hot sand to give a shaded effect to the flowers and leaves, see Plate 8. Further naturalistic effects on flower petals and leaves were obtained by saw cuts which were accentuated by the glue forced through to the surface during the application of the panel to the article of furniture. The practice of engraving the marquetry did not become popular until its revival during the latter part of the eighteenth century. Some of the woods used for natural colour were rosewood, sandal wood, orange and citron, while the lighter effects came from box, holly (the lightest), acacia and sycamore. Most other fruit woods were used and the background was generally walnut. Arabesque or seaweed marquetry, which was sometimes used in conjunction with parquetry, utilised only two woods; box or holly for the pattern and walnut for the background. The patterns were of the finest symmetrical scrollwork, demanding the highest possible degree of skill from the marquetry cutter and relying on the fineness of the work rather than an assortment of colours for its impact.

A type of veneering which was introduced during this period and remained popular well into the 1720s was a method known as quartering, see Fig. 25. It was found that four slices of veneer cut from the same piece of wood naturally had almost identical markings. Although seventeenth and eighteenth century veneers were almost one-eighth and not less than one sixteenth of an inch thick, four slices could be produced by a good veneer cutter or sawyer from well under an inch of timber, allowing for the thickness of the saw. It was also found that the knots, burrs, growths and other irregularities on a tree produced the most attractive veneer. Imagine a cube of timber from which four cuts of veneer have been taken. If, say, the bottom left-hand corners are placed together when the four are laid out to form a large square, the pattern in the wood is not only repeated four times but joins itself at the edges. This method of decoration was employed all over the country, and some charming examples of attractive quartering on country-made furniture, the underneath or inside of which is often very poor quality, can still be found. Incorporated with and finishing off all types of veneering were the stringing, crossbanding and mouldings. Crossbanding is a decorative strip or line of veneer of variable width wherein the grain runs across the line and, during the walnut period, was applied in lengths of seldom more than three to four inches. Taking the same cube of timber used to illustrate quartering, a slice is cut from one side, say half an inch thick. This is then laid flat and cut in the same way as veneer, see Fig. 27A.

An advancement on this was the introduction of feathering or herring-bone crossbanding. For this effect the first cut in the cube was made diagonally approximately one-quarter of an inch thick. Two slices of banding were then cut from this, and when being laid as veneer one was turned over thus producing the herring bone, see Fig. 27B. The mouldings on the drawer fronts of earlier furniture were now being ousted by the decorative use of veneer, and so the moulding was placed round the edge of the drawer opening on the carcase. This took the form of a raised crossbanding of semi-circular and later semi-oval section, and within a few years a groove was worked in the moulding giving a double semi-circular section, see Plate 9.

1. An oak chest, c. 1600. The front is arcaded in typical Renaissance manner and decorated with 'chip' carving of roundels and flower stalks.

2. Country made walnut chest furniture, 1700-1720. It can be assumed that as the construction of the article below is somewhat crude, it was provincial and is therefore likely to be slightly out of period, i.e. made a few years later than outward appearance might suggest. Although the side runner on the carcase fitting into the deep rabbet in the drawer shown here had been superseded by bottom runners on fashionable furniture by the end of the 17th century, their use continued on provincial furniture for several years into the 18th century. The large double dovetail joint at the drawer front and the single nail are also typical of earlier construction but the fact that the joint is stopped or lapped, i.e., the side of the drawer does not come through to the front of the drawer to be concealed by the veneer, means that it must have been made after 1690, when lapped joints were introduced. The double moulded cross-banding on the carcase suggests c. 1710 and the herring bone banding on the drawer confirms 1710-1720. The gilt brass and engraved escutcheon/plate handle, which is original, is of the type used during the first quarter of the 18th century. The top moulding is correctly made in small pieces seldom more than three to four inches in length across the grain, and the soft wood of the carcase can be seen underneath. The faintly visible horizontal lines on the drawer surface mean that at sometime the article has been repolished but as can be seen on the lower left hand corner, the veneer is at least twice as thick as its 19th century counterpart, see Fakes, page 54.

3. A cedar wood and oak chest, c. 1660. The raised geometric decoration on the front of the deep top drawer and the two doors below was most popular between c. 1650-1665, the austerity of the design lending itself to the general severity of the Commonwealth period. The application of split pillars suggests more freedom which came with the Restoration. At some time during the mid 18th century this chest had bracket feet added to bring it more up to date with contemporary furniture. Following its discovery in 1968, these were carefully removed to reveal the original feet formed by the stiles which also bear the iron hinges for the doors and continue through to the top.

4. *The interior of the lower part of the chest illustrated in Plate 3. The doors swing on iron hinges nailed to the main upright members, called stiles, which on furniture of this period also form the feet. Three long drawers enclosed by the doors are plain except for three blocks of timber simulating a muntin. The centre block has the door lock fastening, and the original iron drop ring handles are typical examples, applied in the correct manner as shown in Fig. 38, on page 58.*

5. *A late 17th century carved and gilt mirror frame, showing considerable European influence in the design of the top cresting. The base incorporates the shell motif which remained popular on the plainer furniture of the Queen Anne period.*

6. A walnut armchair of the early Restoration period, c. 1665. This example shows the use of pierce carving with scallop shell, formal foliage scrolls and flower heads on the front stretcher and the frame for the back panel of canework. This can be seen to be coarse, with large holes. By 1680 the caning was finer with small holes. The H stretcher rails and the fine quality barley sugar twist turning are also indicative of the Restoration period. The carving in low relief on the seat rails, front legs and arm terminals and caps makes this chair a fine example of the period.

7. A small gate leg table, c. 1675. Since the first part of the 16th century small folding tables were known in England, and during the 17th century their advantages were fully recognised. Gate leg tables of all sizes were produced from the second quarter of the 17th century and followed the progress of the turners' designs. Thus they can be dated after the introduction of a particular design; thereafter accuracy is difficult, for such patterns tended to remain popular in the provinces long after they had gone out of fashion in the large towns. This example shows extremely good baluster, ball and ring or bobbin turning, but a fine example might have the rails and stretchers turned to match. A single peg joint is also visible on the outer leg of the gate and the feet are original.

8. *An extremely fine example of floral marquetry applied to a small lace or ruffle box, c. 1680. The stringing, crossbanding and use of all the techniques described on page 31 are seen here. Especially important are the saw cuts through the wood to accentuate the veins of leaves, petals and feathers. The glue which was forced through when the panel was applied has blackened with age and added definition.*

The practice of scribing the surface after its application to achieve the same effect was not done in England until the latter part of the 18th century when marquetry had a revival. Also clearly visible is the shaded effect achieved by dipping each piece of wood into hot sand.

9. *A walnut veneered, deal side table of the William and Mary period, c. 1700. This example illustrates the details described on page 32 and also shows the careful choice and matching of timber. The shaped apron suggests a slightly later date, and the inclusion of the elaborate X stretcher with this points to a country made piece, perhaps a few years out of period.*

10. *The underside of the table shown in Plate 9. The rough hewn surfaces of its inner sides compliment the theory of provincial origin. However, authenticity is unquestionable: the clean appearance of the top planks which, when the drawer is in place, would receive no handling; the darkened edge of the shaped apron from hand and finger grease (a white line here would indicate false staining perhaps sixty years ago); the slight darkening between the side rail and where the drawer side fits shows where some, but not much, dusty air has circulated; a marked darkening on the outer edges of the top; and the extreme reaches of the polishing cloth on the inside of the leg finish in just the right place. See Fakes, page 50.*

11. An early 18th century wing or 'easy' armchair, c. 1720, with walnut curved legs front and back, terminating at front in pad feet and at back with square section. See Fig 33, A and B. Easy chairs with wings, or 'cheeks as they were called, are recorded during the late 17th century but they did not become generally popular until the Queen Anne period.

12. An early George I period bureau cabinet. The top has open shelves with a row of small drawers at the bottom, all enclosed by two mirrored glass doors and surmounted by a flat cornice. Under each door in the cabinet section is a candle slide. The bureau has two short and two long drawers below a false or dummy drawer front which covers a space known as a well. Access to this is inside the sloping front of the bureau and is concealed by a sliding cover which when closed forms part of the writing surface immediately in front of the centre door compartment. The bureau is shown with the sloping front or 'fall open to disclose the centre door compartment, a secret compartment each side hidden by simulated classical columns, pigeon holes and small drawers.

13. *A Queen Anne period kneehole desk or writing table, c. 1710. This clearly shows the two sets of three and one long drawers framing the space to accommodate the knees of the user. The small simulated arch over is also a shallow drawer, and beyond this is a small cupboard with drawer under. All the features on this desk are original and contemporary. Note the bun feet, gilt metal handles and escutcheon plates, the semi-circular moulding at the base and the double moulding round the drawers.*

14. *An early George I period walnut tallboy, c. 1715. The top three long and three short drawer chest with overhanging moulding stands in the original three drawer base on four curved cabriole legs terminating in pad feet. The herring bone banding has moved in from the edge of the drawer leaving a slightly larger margin for cross banding, and the drawer fronts extend beyond the drawer opening. This pattern ran concurrently with inside drawers for some years, to be replaced by a cock bead within a few years.*

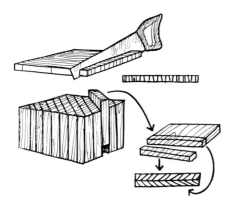

Fig. 27: The method of cutting timber to produce (a) cross banding and (b) herring bone banding.

Almost without exception, herring-bone banding is peculiar to the period of walnut furniture in England, which ran from the Restoration period, from about 1660 to about 1730. The same might be said for crossbanded mouldings, but it must be remembered that fashion did not change overnight, and much furniture of the early mahogany period which began, in country furniture at least, about 1730, was produced with considerable influence of the previous period.

With the continued popularity of decorated furniture, whether lacquered, gilded or veneered, it was obvious that woods cheaper than oak might be used for the construction of the carcase or main body. Pine and deal were used to a great extent, and for veneered furniture especially the large flat surfaces required were formed by glueing planks of these woods side by side. Unfortunately, over the years it has become apparent how unsatisfactory this was, for being softer than oak, both these woods expand and contract to a greater degree and this method of construction gave them no room to do so. Hence the considerable amount of warping and cracking which can be a constant worry to those people lucky enough to own any genuine walnut period furniture today.

The next important development to begin during the late seventeenth century and which by the 1720s had altered forever the construction of our furniture was the production and use of metal screws. The tops of tables and chests which had previously been fastened by pegging through, were now screwed on from underneath. Incisions with a rounded surface were made in the inside of the top rail to accommodate the screw which went into the top at an angle, see Fig. 28. The rounded surface of the incision should be noted, for it was not until the nineteenth

41

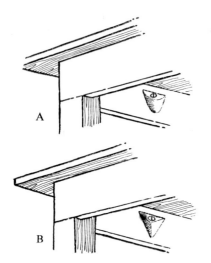

Fig. 28: (a) shows the rounded incision made to accommodate the screw securing the top on an eighteenth century piece of furniture. (b) shows the V shape incision adopted on English furniture during the latter part of the nineteenth century. During the eighteenth century many side, console and pier tables had marble tops; over the years these were often replaced with wooden tops which had to be screwed on. If the only incisions for screws in the underside of the frieze rail are V shaped the top is likely to have been fixed during the nineteenth century.

century that V incisions for this purpose were made on English furniture.

By the end of the seventeenth century the different articles of furniture in use in our middle and upper class houses had become as varied as the types of people who commissioned their manufacture. But one article in particular that had become standard household equipment was the tea table.

Although tea had been known in England since the early part of the seventeenth century, it was not until the late 1690s that it really began to affect our furniture industry. Tea was first noted in this country as having medicinal qualities, being a preventative against disease and a remarkable cure for hangovers. Naturally there were many who disapproved its use, viewing with disdain those high in social circles who had gained the habit of taking tea after dinner rather than a bottle and a pipe. Tea was shipped to this country in measures of a certain weight. The measure was a *kati* which equalled just over a pound avoirdupois, and so many containers each holding this weight were packed into chests for transportation. As the popularity of tea grew, so first the chests and then the *kati* boxes themselves became decorated. The *katis* were usually of tin, either lightly engraved in the Chinoiserie manner or Japanned. The early chests had hinged lids and were mostly covered with fine morocco leather and embellished with silver and/or gilt metal hinges, corners and locks.

42

Fig. 29: A rectangular tray top tea table in the style of the early eighteenth century. This type of table remained popular until the middle of the century when the tripod table gained favour.

Within a few years miniature chests made by the cabinet maker and containing up to three miniature *katis* for the home blending of the different sorts of tea being imported became increasingly popular. During the eighteenth century these small tea chests of single, double or triple compartments were made of all manner of materials by all manner of people. Toward the end of the eighteenth century the name changed from chest to 'caddy', derived from the original *kati*. Great ceremony was accorded to the drinking of tea, and despite its then prohibitive cost, it appears to have become very much a national habit by the end of the seventeenth century. In 1700 the Joiners' Company, in a case against the Import of Manufactured Furniture and Cabinet Work, complained that apart from the vast quantities of cabinets, chests, trunks, screens and chairs being unloaded at the Port of London by the East India merchants, over six thousand five hundred lacquered tea tables had been imported within the previous four years. A tax of 15% was subsequently put on all such merchandise, but the number shows just how popular tea drinking had become, and it is perhaps a reflection on the quality of the imported tea tables that apparently not one is known to have survived. The earliest examples of English made tea or china tables are rectangular with a dished or sunken top and, being intended for use in any part of the room, are equally decorated on all four sides, see Fig. 29.

Before the end of the seventeenth century several other changes in the needs and uses of domestic furniture occurred which were to affect the furniture industry thereafter. One was the considerable use of the small single drawer side table. A typical example of a provincial or country-made side table of the William and Mary period is shown in Plate 9. The crudely

43

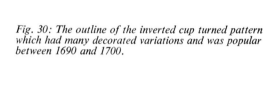

Fig. 30: The outline of the inverted cup turned pattern which had many decorated variations and was popular between 1690 and 1700.

made top of two rough hewn planks of deal (see Plate 10) bears a finely quartered pegged-on top of matched walnut veneer incorporating the use of herring bone banding to frame the edges and create an oval in the centre. The outer edge is banded but not crossbanded, which was done to accentuate the crossbanding on the moulded lip. The drawer front and frieze are veneered through with walnut cut in the same way as oyster-shell, the line of the drawer being shown with a single band of herring bone banding. The frieze, even on most country furniture of this period, has become shaped. On contemporary chairs this shaped frieze effect was gained by the use of ornate and heavy fringes at the edges of the upholstery material which by now covered front and side rails as well as the seat. The shape of the stretcher illustrated is also similar to that of the chairs of the period, but a disappointing lack of decoration, under such a fine top, suggests the table was essentially a domestic article probably made for the servants' quarters in a fine house. The legs, too, might add weight to this supposition. Although the lower part with the straight tapering shape is all that could be desired, had the table been of great quality the top part would have had the inverted cup shape, see Fig. 30, which required much larger pieces of timber for turning. The bun feet are also typical of this period, going out of fashion at the beginning of the eighteenth century.

Another similar type of table to become very popular at this time was the dressing or toilet table. Since as early as the four-teenth century both men and women had used considerable quantities of cosmetics and make-up, but it is unclear whether or not pieces of furniture were specially made to contain the numerous paints, powders, salves, hair dyes, perfumes, brushes, combs, etc. until the seventeenth century. However, during the late seventeenth century, when people actually died from applying too much make-up with a white lead or mercury base, toilet tables and toilet sets are specifically mentioned. Their design is similar to that of the side table until the 1720s, except that the single shallow drawer was narrower and extra space was provided by a deep drawer at each end accommodated in a more deeply shaped frieze, see Fig. 31. From the beginning of the eighteenth century it was usual to have a dressing table made with a matching toilet mirror which stood on the top; this was a simply framed mirror plate connected to two upright supports by two swivel screws, and supported on a box type base containing one or two rows of small drawers, see Fig. 32.

Fig. 31: A three drawer dressing table of the early eighteenth century type. The curved legs, shown here terminating in pad feet, should continue through to the top forming the corner stiles of the carcase frame and could be of solid oak, walnut, or after 1725, mahogany.

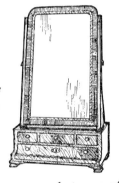

Fig. 32: A walnut period box base toilet mirror, 1710. The crossbanded frame has a narrow gilt inside border and swings on two fixing screws. This shape of base, sometimes with a single row of drawers, or a single drawer, was popular throughout the first half of the eighteenth century.

During the eighteenth century furniture was made to one of three main standards. First, the extremely fine and fashionable pieces made by appointed craftsmen for the royal courts and households, and the great country houses of the wealthy aristocracy; second, the vast quantity of articles made in London, other cities and major provincial towns for the houses of the moderately wealthy artisan and squire class; third, the cottage furniture made by the village carpenter or retained joiner on a large estate to furnish the houses of the villagers or tenants.

The furniture industry was to expand and flourish in an age of a complex pattern of fashions and designs sometimes changing rapidly, sometimes running concurrently. It was encouraged by the growth of population, internal prosperity and technical advancement and unrestrained by political and religious influence. It was also an age of trade publications. Leading manufacturers and designers produced and sold books of their designs which were copied by craftsmen throughout the land as well as their skill, materials available and the money at their disposal would allow. The pattern had been set during the reign of William III by his designer, Daniel Marot. In 1684, the year before the Revocation of the Edict of Nantes, Daniel Marot, a Huguenot, left his native France to seek asylum in Holland. He was already well known as an architect and furniture designer and before long was working for William, Prince of Orange. In 1694 Marot came to England and continued working under the royal patronage. He is probably best known for his designs of corner chimney pieces with graduated shelves above, but these were only one example of his adaptations from the heavy and ornate Louis XIV style. A book of Daniel Marot's designs published in the early eighteenth century shows considerable use of elaborate drapery for curtains, bed hangings, chairs and stools. His designs for the 'show wood' parts of furniture advocate much ornate carving with amorini or cherubs, masks, torsos and figures, at the same time incorporating many of the patterns already mentioned such as the bow or hoop stretcher rail, the inverted cup and straight taper turning and the curved front leg, see Fig. 33A.

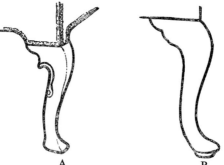

A   B

Fig. 33: The curved leg, introduced and becoming popular in England during the early eighteenth century. The square section foot (a) preceded the round pad foot (b) but continued with it until 1725.

THE EIGHTEENTH CENTURY

Queen Anne, 1702-1714

Two years after the turn of the century, William III died and Anne, second daughter of James II, succeeded to the throne in her thirty-seventh year. She was a thoroughly good woman, gentle, amiable and kind. Hers was the period of great victories on the Continent—we were once again at war with France—under the leadership of John Churchill, Duke of Marlborough. His wife Sarah Jennings was also an important figure, for she had considerable influence over the Queen. It was an age of great statesmen and great men of literature, and in 1706-7 the final Union of England and Scotland. In our furniture history we had the beginning of a combination of comfort and elegance in general middle class articles. For the first time the backs of chairs were shaped in solid wood to fit the body of the sitter.

Fig. 34: A walnut chair in the style popular from 1710 to c. 1730. The solid wood back splat is shaped for added comfort. The generous sweep of the back frame is apparent in the arms and was often repeated in the shape of the seat frame. Stretcher rails are rarely found on chairs of this pattern, but reappeared on fashionable furniture after the 1750s.

A large centre splat of stylised vase shape was supported by a curved frame, and the seat frame continued this shape by ballooning out towards the front, see Fig. 34. Fully upholstered wing armchairs were popular, with deep cushions in the seats, and on short curved legs at the front and splay legs at the back, see Plate 11. We were now using English as well as imported walnut, and a taste for less ornate decoration accentuated the importance of good design and careful choice of timber. However, one popular carved motif of the period was the scallop shell which was used to decorate the friezes, front rails, and to cap the knees of the curved legs on all types of furniture. The curved leg in the form it took during the Queen Anne period was the introduction of what we now know as the cabriole leg. Cabriole was a French dancing term meaning a bound or leap, and was therefore used to describe legs on furniture which terminated in a simulated animal's foot below the curved knee. This had developed from the Flemish moulded curve with either the Braganza or animal's foot incorporating the shaped moulded stretcher. During the early part of the eighteenth century the curve of the knee became simplified and often terminated in a simple pad foot, see Fig. 33B. The additional strength of this design soon became apparent and the heavy moulded stretcher disappeared.

By this time the interior arrangements of houses had begun to change. The use of large tall windows, imposing fireplaces and doorways required furniture of the same proportions to achieve a balanced effect. Although it was not until the 1720s that this became truly fashionable largely due to the work of William Kent, console or pier tables with tall mirrors over (pier glasses) were already being made. Also, in rooms other than the library, case furniture became taller and narrower.

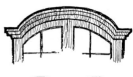

Fig. 35: Three examples of cornice shapes that were fashionable during the first quarter of the eighteenth century.

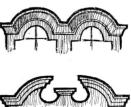

A typical example of this was the development of the bureau-cabinet, of which the earliest types were made in three main parts. The top part of an escritoire, with its deeply sloping front enclosing several small drawers and compartments, was placed on a low chest of drawers base instead of an open stand. Placed on to the horizontal top part of the escritoire was a double door cupboard, having either solid wood or mirror glass panels, which was surmounted by a shaped cornice which at this time would be single, double dome or flat, see Plate 12. Some typical cornice shapes are illustrated in Fig. 35. In order to make the cupboard 'sit' securely, a substantial moulding was placed around the edge of the escritoire. A similar moulding was placed round the chest/escritoire joint and large metal carrying handles were often fixed on the sides of all three pieces. The feet would be turned bun shape, or later a plain bracket. Some examples of both the bureau and the bureau-cabinet of this period have the base constructed with a row of small drawers placed one above another each side of a recessed compartment which accommodated the knees of the writer. This same construction was used for some types of knee-hole dressing tables and the flat top knee-hole writing desk, see Plate 13. The recessed compartment soon disappeared from the bureau, however, for the open lid or 'fall' provided ample space for knees, but the compartment was then difficult to reach. So most walnut period bureaux have three long drawers below a deep top rail sometimes decorated to simulate a drawer front. The space behind this dummy drawer was accessible only by opening the fall which could be locked. Inside, a portion of the top slid back underneath the small drawers and compartments revealing the well. This characteristic disappeared during the 1730s and the space was filled with a proper drawer. Another article which first gained general popularity during the early 1700s was the tallboy. This version of a chest on chest invariably had the bottom drawer arrangement and rail similar to that of the dressing table, with the cabriole legs made suitably shorter, see Plate 14.

George I, 1714-1727

George I was born in 1660, created Duke of Cambridge 1706, proclaimed King in 1714, and was crowned at Westminster later that year. He was the first sovereign of the House of Hanover, being the son of the Elector of Hanover and Sophia, grand-daughter of James I. Apart from a Jacobite rising in 1715, and the well-known financial 'South Sea Bubble' the reign of George I was peaceful. Possibly through the lack of personal effect of the King on designs and fashions, coupled with the increased ability of larger sections of the community to afford fashionable houses and furnishings, the leading styles from the early years of George I to about 1800 are generally recognised by the name of the style or its designer instead of the name of the reigning monarch. For example, we refer to Rococo rather than George II; to Hepplewhite or Adam rather than George III, see charts on pages 60 and 61.

From 1710 to 1720 design in general mellowed. A combination of the best features of the previous fifteen years produced a subtle, functional and attractive style of furniture. The outlines formed the basis for many of the elaborate designs of the 1740s and 1750s, and can often be discerned under the extravagant decoration of the Rococo period. The Queen Anne style prevailed well into the 1720s, as if our cabinet makers needed a break to settle down and prepare themselves for the expansive times ahead. The Palladian, Rococo, Gothic Revival and second Chinoiserie styles were to lift some from craftsmen status to high society, making them extremely wealthy in the process. The great age of English furniture had begun.

FAKES, ALTERATIONS, IMPROVEMENTS

The title of this chapter summarises the main types of spurious articles likely to be encountered today. An increase in demand for any merchandise inevitably leads at some point to the production of inferior facsimiles, and old English furniture is certainly no exception. This is no new situation. The work of carvers, cabinet makers and polishers of the early 1900s is a memorial to the enthusiastic but inexpert collectors and the unethical or ignorant vendors of that period. Therefore today we not only have to be aware of the skilled faker and reproducer of the present time but the work of such men since the turn of the century. To complicate matters even more there are the items brought up to date in appearance or altered in shape and use by enthusiastic amateurs during the late Victorian period. During the 1860s the Warwick School of Carving popularised a style of extremely high quality but over-elaborate carved decoration on furniture. This rapidly became a fashionable hobby for middle and upper class citizens in Victorian society who were undoubtedly responsible for the massacre of many fine pieces of early oak. But in an age of tremendous industrial development little respect was shown to ordinary household articles of a past era, and to recarve such items was a means of practice and therefore a justifiable improvement. However, their motives were at least honest if completely misguided. In contrast, during the early 1900s the services of the skilled faker were in demand to appease the appetites of wealthy collectors of the antique. Having obtained the finest known examples available, these men sought the unknown and the impossible. Furniture made to designs undreamt of by Kent, Chippendale and Hepplewhite was forced into famous collections through various channels by pitting the pride of one collector against another. Inevitably several law suits followed during the 1920s bringing disrepute to all concerned. But to be fair, few of the collectors and their advisers had dealings with bow-front chests, pot cupboards, washstands and the like. Not for them the utility article which is an important part if not the basis for a thorough knowledge of furniture and its construction.

The complete fake is an article made with old materials, in the old method of construction by a highly skilled cratsman and produced for the sole purpose of deception. The majority of fakes of this description were made during the early part of this century, and having had over fifty years genuine wear and tear their discovery can sometimes be difficult. But while the skilled fakers had a knowledge of the design and styles of the early periods, being naturally proud of their work, few resisted the temptation of incorporating a small feature somewhere on the article, almost like a trademark. This might be a minor addition or omission which would not have occurred on the genuine piece. A fact which may well have confused the original purchaser is that these fakes were fine articles which, had they been genuine, would have been treated with respect throughout their lifetime and therefore not expected to show signs of constant use. But once exposed as false, reverence ceased, and half a century of daily handling has added enough appearance of age to confuse the furnishing collector of today, for a most important guide to the recognition of a fake is the evidence of use. For many years now the production of this type of fake has been low, the cost of skilled labour and the scarcity of the correct materials making it financially unworthwhile. Unfortunately the same cannot be said for the next category, the basically old but improved piece. This describes an article which, while remaining structurally unaltered, has the addition of decoration which would have been applied to only its finest contemporary counterpart. In general terms it describes a plain article converted by decoration into what appears to be a fine article. This was done mostly on eighteenth century mahogany furniture, but there are instances of this type of improvement occurring on country-made walnut furniture of the early eighteenth century.

The next hazard to confront the present day collector is easy to discern, but it leads directly to the type of copy most encountered today: the reproduction. The commercial mass-produced reproduction is made as near as possible to the designs of the antique, being slightly modified for use in the modern home and made with the latest and most up-to-date machinery. This type has been made since the turn of the century, but its very design and proportion are enough to give it away at first or, at most, second glance. The commercial reproduction was never intended to deceive, but to fulfil a demand for a style or fashion for the antique while remaining available in cost equivalent to any modern furniture of the time. However, vast quantities of extremely fine quality reproduction furniture have been and are being produced. These pieces are exact replicas of an original, with the minimum use of machinery in the production. Considerable time and skill is employed in research for authenticity of design and the achievement of a suitable patina, but the use of new timber and the absence of any signs of age underneath the article are sufficient for immediate recognition.

The article which has been altered structurally exists, like the recarved or improved piece, for one of two reasons. Furniture was altered during the nineteenth century because its original function was inadequate or because it was the wrong size for a certain position in the house. Bureau cabinets and bookcases were separated, sideboards reduced in width or length, clothes presses were made into wardrobes by removing the shelves. During the twentieth century, such alterations continued, but more often to falsely increase the value as refurnishing with antiques became more popular.

Having established the types of fakes most likely to be encountered the next step is to realise the various ways they can be identified. Unfortunately most of the unhelpful remarks inferring that years of study and practical experience are the only ways to learn are for the most part true. However, there are several guides rather than rules which may help to establish whether or not an article needs further examination. The most important single aspect in learning about old furniture is the ability to recognise that something is wrong. Knowing exactly what or where will come with time and experience, and when faced with such a problem piece there should be no hesitation in seeking further authoritative advice. It is equally important to avoid being too hasty in condemning outright an article where some doubt exists. The reason may be no more than an honestly but poorly executed repair. Providing this is not excessive and does not alter the character or use of the article it may be acceptable.

When viewing furniture formulate and memorise knowledge into brackets or headings which can be brought to mind quickly and easily.

For example:— Date + Shape + Use + Material.
Colour and surface condition (patina).   Signs of wear.
Construction.   Wood behaviour.   Unexposed wood condition.

The first four should be compatible and contemporary and will signify the earliest date an article could have been made, i.e.: Rococo style *after* 1730, tea tables *after* 1680, walnut *after* 1655. Having established that date, shape, use and material are contemporary, look for colour and surface condition.

Patina
Since craftsmen first took pride in their work, the outer

surfaces of furniture have had some sort of preservative treatment when new. Following the decline in popularity during the sixteenth century of painting furniture after the application of a grain filler, the use of either an oil polish or a polish of beeswax and turpentine became standard practice. Through oxidisation the oil polish darkened the wood, whereas the beeswax sealed it and retained the mellow colour. This accounts for the majority of oak furniture being of two distinct colour types, dark and light. It is accepted that there were definite regional preferences for the colour of furniture when new; for instance, that from the south is generally lighter than that from the midlands. The use of oil or wax polish continued on country furniture until the nineteenth century, but during the early Restoration period the use of varnish became most popular on all fine furniture. This remained so until the advent of French polishing, an easier and inferior method of obtaining an immediate lustrous surface, during the 1820s. The first type of varnish used on fine furniture since the latter part of the sixteenth century was an oil and resin varnish. Thin coats of this mixture were applied to the surface of the wood, allowing time between each for the resin to dry out the oil. The surface was then rubbed with any one of a variety of mild abrasives which eventually filled the grain and left the timber well preserved, of good colour and ready for the first beeswaxing. Oil varnish was superseded in the early 1660s by a spirit varnish. This consisted of spirits of wine and gum lac known as China varnish and was introduced to England from the East where it had been used to preserve the fine lacquer work being imported into England at that time. As with the lacquer work itself, the materials were not available in western Europe to make China varnish, but before long we had discovered a suitable alternative. This was basically the same formula with a spirit base but either seed-lac or shell-lac was used instead of gum lac. The method of application was essentially the same as for the oil varnish.

Whether a piece of oak has the golden brown or the deep dark colour it should have good patination. This describes the condition of the surface after years of waxing with beeswax, the accumulation of grease and dirt and the multitude of small scratches resulting from general but not careless use. Over a long period of time dirt and wax have not only filled the grain but have built up into small ridges above the surface. These can be clearly seen when viewed obliquely against the light and cannot be reproduced, thus providing a guarantee of at least an old top, leg, rail or stretcher. Whether or not it belongs to the article in question is another consideration. Signs of careless use such as inkstains, bleached spots, obvious scratches, bruises and worn edges can all be reproduced in a process known as 'distressing'. See page 55. Walnut has a much closer grain than oak and the raised grain is not so prominent in old patina. But as most flat surfaces of fashionable furniture of the late seventeenth century were veneered we are presented with an alternative guide. On an original walnut veneered surface the glue can be seen to have oozed out between the joints of the veneer and can be perceived perhaps easier with the fingertips than with the eye. This is particularly noticeable on marquetry decoration where the pattern is outlined by this 'raised grain' effect. On seventeenth century marquetry the additional details of veins on leaves, feathers on birds, etc., which appear to have been scribed on to the wood are, in fact, fine saw cuts. The lines are accentuated by the glue being forced through from underneath when the veneer was first laid. English marquetry was never enhanced with surface drawing until the second great marquetry period following the Classical Revival of Robert Adam in the 1760s.

Signs of wear

Whereas the signs of use in the patina concern the outer surfaces, signs of wear relate to the effects of handling and the movements of working parts. Most early oak and walnut furniture originally stood on a stone floor that was frequently washed with water. Water will gradually rot wood and so one would expect to see signs of the feet having been eaten away and discoloration three to four inches up each leg. However, when the feet became unsteady it was common practice to cut them off as far as necessary and some early stools and chairs have the bottom rails at floor level due to this. Unfortunately a great many more have had the feet replaced and often so badly that true restoration is difficult. In order to examine the feet of a piece of furniture it has to be lifted up or tilted. When doing this note where the hands automatically take hold and where the ends of the fingers touch. It will be moved in the same way it has been moved since it was made and the hands and fingers will reach the same area. Such places should be darker than the rest of the underside. The natural oils of hands and fingers and the gradual accumulation of dust and dirt will have given the appearance of almost a patina. The rest of the underside should be dry looking, paler and perhaps dusty but not stained or polished. This applies without exception to chair and stool rails, drawer linings and table frames. Close scrutiny of the movement of working parts where two wood surfaces rub one against another should always reveal corresponding friction marks. The underneath of gate-leg table leaves where the leg pulls out in an arc to support the leaf, drawers and their runners and hinged doors that have fractionally dropped and rub on the frame or rail are typical instances.

While the faker seems to have ignored the simulation of hand holds underneath furniture, he has certainly spared no effort and imagination in achieving an instant patina on the outer surfaces or show wood. The effects of discoloration of most timbers can be gained by using chemicals. For the country faker in the past the most popular and efficient method of achieving age and in particular the rotted away feet and watermark appearance was to stand the furniture in a regularly used stable. The acidity therein speeded the work of two hundred years into a matter of a few months. All manner of implements such as chains, small pieces of clinker as well as the conventional tools of the workshop were used to obtain the bruises and scratches that occur with constant use and form an integral part of the patina. But here, too, the enthusiastic faker so often gives himself away by overdoing the 'distressing'. This occurs when signs of use appear on places where it would not be expected and closer inspection reveals the distressing to be too regular in pattern.

Wood behaviour

As explained on page 9 the willow pegs should remain protruding from the inside top rails of English seventeenth century seat furniture, while their outside ends should be almost level with the surface of the leg or top. Not quite level, for timber contracts across the grain not along it. Therefore the peg might be fractionally smaller in diameter but it will be no shorter. The leg will have reduced in the same way, leaving the willow peg protruding just above the surface. This contraction applies to a greater or lesser degree to all timber and can be a useful guide, particularly when viewing country or very early furniture when often less well seasoned and matured woods were used. This is especially true and evident on farm house type oak tables with clamped ends. It is always good to see the clamps or cross members a little longer than the width of the top, see Fig. 36, for the top will have shrunk across and so fractionally will the clamps but their lengths will have remained the same.

Decoration

The fact that the decoration of an article is contemporary in design is insufficient evidence of its authenticity. For example, the carved shell found on rail or knee of most good quality Queen Anne furniture was a natural motif for the carver to reproduce on an originally plain article. When an eighteenth century chairmaker planned to decorate his chair with carving he allowed sufficient timber for the motif to stand proud of

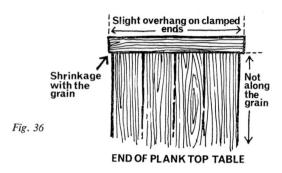

Slight overhang on clamped ends

Shrinkage with the grain

Not along the grain

Fig. 36

END OF PLANK TOP TABLE

the outline of the leg or rail, see Fig. 37. The recarver or faker had no such opportunity, and had therefore to cut into the timber to give the impression of relief. If the carving does not appear raised above the outline of a curved surface it is unlikely to be contemporary. For many years antique walnut furniture has commanded a higher price than oak, and many early oak bureaux and chests have been decorated with walnut veneer for that reason. However, with the exception of clock cases and pieces of the finest quality, English furniture of the seventeenth and early eighteenth century walnut period was rarely made with walnut veneered on to oak. Any part visible, such as drawer linings and legs, should be solid and not veneered. Pine and deal were used for the carcases and drawer backs of veneered furniture and any piece found contrary to this is usually not English or of a later date. The veneer should be thick, being saw cut, see page 32, for it was not until the nineteenth century that thin knife cut veneer was produced.

During the last hundred years many two part pieces of furniture such as tallboys, bureau bookcases and cabinets have been separated; and many originally single pieces have had upper parts added. This was often done without thought or care for the original, thus providing several points to look for. Such two-piece furniture evolved from the cabinet or chest on stand of the late seventeenth century and the method of securing the top to the bottom remained unchanged. The stand had a retaining moulding on each side and the front to contain the base of the cabinet, see Fig. 39. The moulding was seldom applied to the cabinet, and the top of the base which was to receive the cabinet was rarely veneered. When a chest of drawers was made as a dressing chest the top was intended to be used and visible and therefore decorated with veneer. When the same structure was made as the upper part of a tallboy the top was too high to be seen and therefore not veneered. Many top parts of tallboys have had feet added to make them into fashionable small chests, but the proportions of the large overhanging moulding at the top edge, and the similar moulding at the base which has to be made to balance, should be enough to arouse suspicion even if the top has been veneered at the time of its alteration.

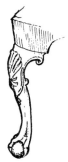

Fig. 37: A curved leg of the walnut or early mahogany period showing the carving on the knee standing proud of the outline of the curve, and the bold well formed claw and ball foot. When an article has been recarved at a later date the carving has to be below the surface of the curve.

Early eighteenth century handles or pulls were of the pendant, back plate and split pin type. These needed only a small hole in the centre of the drawer to take the tag and might have a small dent or pin hole ¾in. above and below the hole inside the drawer where the tag was fastened, see Fig. 38. During the nineteenth century it was fashionable to remove any old metal handles and replace them with turned wood knobs. This type of handle originated during the last part of the eighteenth century but of much finer proportions than the bulbous creations applied ninety years later. The Victorian wood knob required a large hole, up to ½in. diameter, which can be seen inside the drawer, and was sometimes fixed by a screw thread worked into the drawer and turned on to the shank of the knob. To replace handles of the correct style this large hole has first to be plugged, an operation which is impossible to disguise. Nor should there be need to try. A new handle of original style is preferable to a Victorian one of the wrong size, shape and pattern.

Woodworm

The evidence of woodworm is not necessarily a sign of age in furniture. The woodworm belongs to the same species as the death watch beetle and generally attacks furniture in poorly ventilated conditions. Woodworms eat into timber leaving small round holes visible on the surface. They then change direction and rest just below the surface where they go through various phases of development before emerging. Eggs are laid in the spring and the greatest activity is during the summer months. Use of a well known worm killer is the best treatment, but for

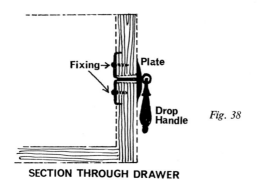

Fixing→

Plate

Drop Handle

Fig. 38

SECTION THROUGH DRAWER

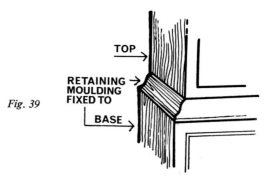

TOP →

RETAINING → MOULDING FIXED TO

BASE →

Fig. 39

severe damage an expert should be consulted. Woodworms burrow in and out of timber, never along the surface, so when any part of a piece of furniture has the surface disfigured with semi-circular channels and worm holes it must have been cut from timber previously used on another piece of furniture. No cabinet maker would have used ugly timber originally, but in an attempt to give 'age' to a piece the faker might.

The points discussed in this chapter are some of the faults likely to be encountered today on furniture of the oak and walnut periods. No one guide should be used alone but in conjunction with the text of the previous chapters and as many other aspects as possible. The inclusion or omission of one feature does not mean that an article is definitely genuine or fake: for instance, the lack of patina with the raised grain effect may have been caused by an enthusiastic polisher in the nineteenth century with no intent to deceive; alternatively its presence means only that the timber has always been the outer surface of something. A sense of proportion plays a large part in recognising that something is wrong, for however elaborate the decoration, furniture of the seventeenth and eighteenth centuries is always well balanced. It cannot be stressed too strongly that knowledge of the original is of paramount importance.

Domestic English furniture was intended for use as well as decoration. Therefore it is only to be expected that working parts such as drawer runners, locks, hinges and wood joints have become worn or damaged. Honest repair or replacement of such damage is quite acceptable providing it is well done, for furniture should, as far as possible, fulfil its original purpose. Treated with normal care and respect, old furniture can add warm atmosphere and character to a home, and most important of all, it will continue to improve in appearance while providing the owner with a pleasing and tangible piece of English history.

Monarch	Date	Style	Materials
HENRY VIII	1509-1547	**TUDOR PERIOD** Gothic Ecclesiastical Renaissance Designs	**OAK** FRUIT WOODS · BEECH · ASH · ELM FOR COUNTRY FURNITURE
EDWARD VI	1547-1553		LOW RELIEF CARVING · SOME PAINT (TEMPERA) & GUILDING
MARY I	1553-1558		
ELIZABETH	1558-1603	**ELIZABETHAN PERIOD** Renaissance	INLAY USING FRUIT WOODS BEECH · ASH · HOLLY · SYCAMORE BONE · IVORY · MOTHER OF PEARL
JAMES I	1603-1625	**STUART PERIOD** Jacobean	
CHARLES I	1625-1649	Renaissance Classicism Dutch Influence	TAPESTRY MANUFACTUREY AT MORTLAKE ESTBD 1620
COMMONWEALTH	1649-1660	Puritan Style	**WALNUT**
RESTORATION	1660	**CAROLEAN PERIOD** Restoration Period	CANE FOR SEATS & BACKS OF CHAIRS · VENEER PARQUETRY OYSTERWOOD · LABURNUM · BOX HOLLY · FLORAL MARQUETRY
CHARLES II	1649-1685	1st Chinoiserie Spanish Influence Netherlands	USING HOLLY · FRUIT WOODS BURR WALNUT · EBONY ETC
JAMES II	1685-1689	Huguenot Influence	CARVED LIME & PINE FOR GESSO & GILDING · SILVERING ORIENTAL ENGLISH LACQUER
WILLIAM III MARY	1689-1702	Dutch Influence	ARABESQUE "SEAWEED" MARQUETRY USING BOX OR HOLLY & WALNUT
ANNE	1702-1714	Baroque	SOLID WALNUT
GEORGE I	1714-1727	**GEORGIAN PERIOD** Palladian Revival Baroque	**MAHOGANY** JAMAICAN · CUBAN
GEORGE II	1727-1760	Roccoco Gothic 2nd Chinoiserie	HONDURAS
GEORGE III	1760-1820	**CLASSICAL REVIVAL** French Taste **REGENCY PERIOD**	PAINTED FURNITURE SATINWOOD · KINGWOOD ETC EXOTIC WOODS FOR VENEERS MARQUETRY REVIVAL
REGENCY	1811-1820	Græco Roman Neo-Classical	
GEORGE IV	1820-1830	Empire · Trafalgar 3rd Chinoiserie Egyptian	GILDING · LACQUER & BUHL
WILLIAM IV	1830-1837	Old French · Gothic Early English Revival	
VICTORIA	1837-1901	**VICTORIAN PERIOD** Gothic (Mediæval) · Rustic Modern English · Art Nouveau Japanese	VARIOUS MATERIALS · PAPIER MACHE
EDWARD VII	1901-1910	**EDWARDIAN PERIOD** Queen Anne, Sheraton Chippendale Style Reproductions	

Time chart of styles and materials

Principal Designers	**Principal Makers**

Principal Designers

INIGO JONES 1573·1651
THE ENGLISH PALLADIO' ONE TIME SURVEYOR GENERAL OF
ROYAL BUILDINGS TO JAMES I & CHARLES I

FRANCIS CLEYN
DESIGNER AT MORTLAKE 1623-1658

DANIEL MAROT Circa 1662·1752

Wm KENT 1686·1748 (Palladian)

Thos CHIPPENDALE 1718·1779
1ST EDITION OF HIS GENTLEMANS & CABINET MAKERS DIRECTOR
PUBLISHED 1754 2ND 1755 3RD 1763

Robt ADAM 1728·1792
CLASSICAL INFLUENCE FOLLOWING HIS RETURN TO ENGLAND
IN **1758**

BATTY & THOS LANGLEY
PUBLISHED IN 1740· CITY & COUNTRY BUILDERS & WORKMANS
TREASURY OF DESIGNS · FRENCH STYLE & GOTHIC

Geo HEPPLEWHITE ·· 1786
1ST EDITION OF HIS THE CABINET MAKERS & UPHOLSTERERS GUIDE
PUBLISHED 1788, 2ND 1789. 3RD 1794

Thos SHERATON 1751·1806
1ST EDITION OF HIS 'THE CABINET MAKERS & UPHOLSTERERS
DRAWING BOOK PUBLISHED 1791-1794

INCE & MAYHEW 1758·1810
1759-63 PUBLISHED 'UNIVERSAL SYSTEM OF HOUSEHOLD
FURNITURE

HENRY HOLLAND 1746·1806
ARCHITECT· STRICT GRAECO·ROMAN STYLE.

Thos HOPE 1769·1831
PUBLISHED HOUSEHOLD FURNITURE & INTERIOR DECORATION
1807

Geo SMITH Circa 1780·1840
PUBLISHED 'A COLLECTION OF DESIGNS FOR HOUSEHOLD
FURNITURE & AND INTERIOR DECORATION 1808

LE GAIGNEUR Circa 1815

AUGUSTUS WELBY PUGIN 1812·1852
GOTHIC DECORATION ON HOUSES OF PARLIAMENT

T. KING
PRODUCED 'THE MODERN STYLE OF CABINET WORK 1839
LIKENED TO DESIGNS BY GEORGE SMITH AND THE LATER
EGYPTIAN' TASTE & CABINET WORK SUPPLEMENT

H.W. & A. ARROWSMITH
'HOUSE DECORATOR & PAINTERS GUIDE ALL STYLES 1840

HENRY WHITTAKER Circa 1847 DESIGNER

Chas EASTLAKE 1836·1906
HINTS ON HOUSEHOLD TASTE

BRUCE TALBERT DESIGNER·APPEARANCE OF
'MEDIAEVAL' WOODWORK PEGGED JOINTS ETC

RICHARD CHARLES DESIGNER

E.W.GODWIN DESIGNER

CHRISTOPHER DRESSER JAPANESE TASTE

Principal Makers

GERREIT JENSEN Circa 1680·1715
CABINET MAKER TO THE ROYAL HOUSEHOLDS
OF CHARLES II & QUEEN ANNE

JOHN GUMLEY 1694·1729

JAMES MOORE 1708·1726

ANDRÉ CHARLES BOULE 1642·1732

Thos CHIPPENDALE 1718·1779

Thos CHIPPENDALE Jnr 1749·1822
IN PARTNERSHIP WITH THOMAS HAIG 1771 - 1796

MATHIAS LOCK 1740·1769 CARVER
VARIOUS PUBLICATIONS CIRCA 1740-1769   AS WELL

W. & J. HALFPENNY Circa 1750
ARCHITECTS & DESIGNERS OF FURNITURE
GOTHIC & CHINESE
FATHER & SON WORKING TOGETHER

Geo HEPPLEWHITE ··1786

Wm HALLETT 1707·1781
MOST POPULAR CABINET MAKER DURING REIGN OF
GEORGE II

Wm & John LINNELL Circa 1720·1763

Geo SEDDON 1727· 1801

Wm VILE & JOHN COBB
Circa 1750·1765
A MOST FAMOUS MANUFACTURING PARTNERSHIP

Wm INCE & JOHN MAYHEW
Circa 1758·1810

Robt & Thos GILLOW Circa 1740-1811
MAKERS OF FURNITURE
·LANCASTER & LATER (CIRCA 1760) LONDON

MARSH & TATHAM 1795

LE GAIGNEUR Circa 1815 BUHL WORK
Geo BULLOCK Circa 1817 (BOULE)

T.B. JORDAN WOODCARVING MACHINE 1845

MORRIS, MARSHALL & FAULKNER
& CO 1861

WARWICK SCHOOL OF CARVING
CIRCA 1850
GREAT EXHIBITION 1851 (STARTED)

HOLLAND & SONS
23 MOUNT STREET · LONDON· EXHIBITED AT
INTERNATIONAL EXHIBITIONS
PARIS 1855.1867· LONDON 1862· 1871

J.G. GRACE & SONS 1745·1899 FAMILY FIRM

Time chart of principal designers and makers

INDEX

A number which is printed in italics refers to the page where an illustration appears.

Printed by Maund & Irvine Ltd., Tring, Herts.